A Scoundrel Ineffable

Relinquishment

Thomas David Karstetter

Made with ♥ on the BookLeaf Publishing Platform

www.bookleafpub.in

www.bookleafpub.com

Dedication

My Empathy Stricken
Brotherhood Lenny Kravitz

And

To the best of the best Jesus of
Nazareth

Preface

Tawdry misshaping happenstance overtly covers antithetical annihilation Proverbially. As I launder stinky foot gestation, I weaken Turlock overbite. All is well in candidacy unknowable.

Acknowledgements

To all the rigamorale disjointed atheists who propose candidacy for literature.

1. SUBMISSIVE TURLOCK UPTICK

As I look to sunset atheism
recalcitrant victimisation celebrates ramshackle isotope
In memory of Christine Kane
A blockchain algorithm undoes chapter five
A tight fisted salesman taints undergrowth
Apoplectic misfit anoints district eight
I seethe indiscretionary as I look to sedate Charleston
Chew
Love enumerates life giving attack
A treasure trove unobsequious

gestates lenghthy sequence of anatomy
A burp can omit lengthy verbose repertoire
Stylistic can can opens up queer monger
As I look to Scandinavian sentencing
a streak of verbiage whips out learning
A substandard Rockafeller lounge lizard leaps altruistic
Turn about is fair play
Huipil surrogate barks up the wrong ladder
Syndicate feature replicates dogma

Tommy Tutone quacks Mayorga
Lunch wagon atheist

Tons of fun jockular misnombre
Squealer likens misfit allegory rebuttal
Squander wander lust insipid
Tell tale fallout disembarks sojourner
I wreak havoc on placid anointing oil
A beak full of flavor sips up alien nation
Quick séance soothes the common owl

Coffee pot plagiarist harpoons staff
Nuttin' Honey splashes all about Mayorga
As I wheel and deal
misanthropist wakes up
A lockturn atheist awakens
Deceitful reckoning acquiesce undertaking
Poke and play azure blanket
reaps what it sows
I lick up turbid gesture

I lick Mortimer hiccups
A lurid endoscope sequences megalomaniac
Tommy Tutone Hastings underwear speaks alacrity
As I tone down encephalitis I sprinkle anatomy
adornment
Pleistocene relish cualquier
Turn about is fair play
I sequence segundo splashing repertoire inane
Squid suffers angst in adept relocation exercise

Potiphar is minuscule estuary

Orel Hershiser speaks tonal referendum
I squeak sedacious misgiving turbid
My knockwurst salad prenuptial agreement
percolates insufferable madman indifferent
Speakeasy lectern encephalitis magnanimous
overtly misused referendum pendulates indemnified as it
were
Insufferable maniacal twisted overbating repository
tweaks effervescent in hiccuping sequence
Spoon filled soup incantation allows for glandular
reproduction

A round about sequence insufferable
speaks incantation frustration
Alacrity removes vacation destination
Hiccuping sequence denies subversive Weddle Hastings
Scandinavian adornment alleviates sequence indemnified
A scandalous adornment permeates relevant victory
Obsequious engenderment
Turtle dove enactment
One, two, three genuflect

Gesture driven spectacle anoints Jessup
Tixtla periwinkle
Tons of fun beefcake

Gifted insight enigma separates close friends
Suit yourself upright in a shirt and tie
My sphincter relates to indecency
Minuscule affect truculent
I scoop up Tertiary commitment as always
Round up Lickety Split a doctrine insufferable

Turtle mountain bespeaks lighthearted Quigley
I look to Staten Island raking in heartache insufferable
I walk among thieves sprinkling democrat rhapsody
Enlighten me a misfit séance perturbed in knighthood
Skid Row duffle bag happens upon cartoon karaoke
Allude a misfit endorphine lengthwise
suttle but ensconced in heartfelt wig
I fart lengthwise like an arrow headlong
Adjutant misfit alights significant as it were

2. A WINGNUT ENCEPHALITIS MACRAME ENGINE

Tommy Tutone rebuttal
Harry carry sequence of events
Liken unto hearsay

A trabajo intransigent
Mealy mouth thunder
A requiem terror gone apathy

As I relish mealy mouth skepticism,
A pickle prenup hasta luego
Raytheon endorsement

Pick me up detergent
A pickle prenup empties itself altruistic
I date a flatulent spatula, sequencing anatomy

I reverb altruistic
Spandau ballet
trinket dissects round about biscuit

Catatonic mind meld

Sophisticated Reinhold
effervesce mind blowing salesman

Accidental overdose
receding hairline
farfetched euphemism toxicity

Tutone adversary speaks trilogy
As I look to verse Colefax vertebrae submits alfresco
Dirty loophole suspects vermin

3. A RADIANT BEING SURMISES TELEPATHY INDOLENT

Tucumcari submits altruist knighthood in secret

Topsy turvy séance spits cualquier innate

I look to savvy sprinkled with democracy

Whimpering to the Almighty

Wardrobe pontiff precludes adjunct spitoon

A grease monkey spits avarice truculent

Milhouse atones for knockwood lectern

Tutone verbatim celestial sink soaps up doctorate mythical

Wood grain atheist allows for spicy victimisation of a derelict

Congruent bathyscath punches fetal reminiscent
allocation

4. COSEQUIN FETAL POSITION AS I LOOK AT IT

Verbiage anoints distal memory
A fetish subtitled harry carry
endorsement obsequious
As I look to earnest drum beat
a heartfelt recompense

eulogizes obviate sequence
Praetorium manifest ogles right of way
Feast your eyes on this dogma
A hiccup alludes to trident ossuary
A misfit encumbrance

seeks to lemniscate offshoot perturbed
As I look to estuary
I seemingly endorse maleficent dogma to no end
Truculent nay sayer
harpoons aghast

Hortence placates a systematic estuary
Cualuier omits brandishing iron
Safety permits oligarch innocuous

A leaf blower submits
Altruistic encumbrance misfit

A sergeant farts frequently
A banishment misnombre
seeks to alleviate trash
Hypnotical offbeat rhythm
silences Khartoum

A clandestine obsequious engenderment
alleviates sequestered verbiage
As I tuck in séance
I relegate misfit obtuse
Tertiary commitment

Burgermeister madman opens up nay saying
I defeat the purpose
Michelob enactment
predates funky cold Medina
I bob altruist insufferable

Candidate for destruction
As I relocate Salisbury
I anoint dysentary
Seeming reprisal
vindicates inept willow

Tommy Tutone
abates tawdry Van De Kamp
willingly submissive Agnostic celebration
As i look to topsy turvy syndicate algorithm
I dust off San Onofre speakeasy

Bludgeoning stargazer
illicits undergrowth
As I seek to abandon estuary
I seek clandestine inauguration
billowing insufferable marksman

A trundle bed breaks even
As I requisition knighthood
an addict verbalizes sanctity
A mutton breath vanquishes the dragon
piecemeal ludicrous appetite

5. FINNY FLUENT FARCICAL PEPTIDE

Dugout canoe celebrates intrusion
insufferable Internal organ

Shore up glossary insurmountable
Cualquier likens fish wish

umbilical celebration
Dulce de leche

Cualquier arrivederci
Liken unto Sebastian soliloquy

Dust yourself off anatomy
In all arrogance of stupidity

I reallocate favoritism unbequeathed
A Beechnut believer

Tungsten allegory
Omnipresent statutory

I oblivate knockwurst happenings on
Turn about is fair play

Bipedal smokehouse gravy
a lectern homey don't play me

Assiduous allegory
makes referendum speakeasy

Touch and go preposterous goad
liken unto sweetie pie ala mode

Snake like turban
touts melodeon

Breakfast estuary
happens upon discovery

Enactmen officiates delegation
repertoire indiscriminate perturbation

Elastic trombone preaches farfetched jalopy
A coin based partitioner waxes beligerent

Juxtapose illicit wisecrack splendiferous
I submit to erstwhile spanking reluctant as it were

6. CUALQUIER ABSENCE

Two tons of fun abets liverwurst love affair
Immaculate conception dictates noon reticent heritage
I look to farcical fantasy farting on flatulent feces
Funny capitalist seeks fantasy farming eloquent heresy
Puns are intended
A Lapland schism celebrates adulthood
Milhouse haphazard telltale Right Wing marksmanship
Tons of fun a displacement
Lockhaven Connecticut bestial séance predicates Al Gore
Fantasy Five Celest victimisation finally submits to
heresy
Rack and pinon reticent algorithm dissects open ended
argument
Aloof steering obviates moron

As I look to fishing
a séance burps unending
Flatulent Spandau Ballet procreates obtuse wishy washy
knighthood
Retro fitting scum predates amethyst runaround in
Turlock
Aiding and abetting hapazard tool shed dichotomy
Turn about is fair play
Mortimer dove in sinking sales inept

Defunct purveyor celebrates stinkyocity in an act of
office
Predestined glory furnishes feces following adjunct
personnage
Ductile lengthwise serendipity omits lackluster love
affair
I break even as luck would have it
Smitten by Al Gore as always

Insubordinate literature abides as always on Candid
Camera
As I look to fetish
I celebrate monotheist government in inept repository
unabated
Cualquier atonement ignites celebratory Cagney and
Lacey
I fish out sustenance verbatim
fondling Mercy seat reluctance
Captured mercy solicits monogram sweatshirt to the
Almighty
As I whimper out loud I collect rapid nay saying
profundity
My Cabrioldlady collective inebriates scuttlebutt as it
were
Distal memories solicit awakening
Adjunct proposal slithers backwards into defunct
underpinning

I salute monotheistic dogmatic rubbernecking to the
Utmost

Swashbuckling bricka bracka tarnishes soliloquy
Kandahar misfit rhythm parties flagrant misshaping
A rebuttal smokes significant mercy insufficient
Al Gore tarnishes misfit séance
Lockhaven Sotheby's tarnishes market dictatorship
Filibuster knighthood afterwards standiing
Inebriate me in lackluster banishment
As I look to verbiage
megalomaniac tarnishes frequent nay sayings
Remarkable district five farms fallacy disbursement
Rectal thermometer obeys knighthood catatonic being
Tertiary commitment tarnishes victimhood

Enigmatic playwright ponders epithet
As I engender circumstance freewill annunciates
Vladimir Putin
A hardliner relinquishes monotheistic value
Piecemeal regurgitation separates flatulent article of
confusion
Underwear seeks difficult inept wayfare technology
Minuscule truancy lacks verbiage under my oath
Freewill circumstance verbiates linkage simultaneously
A nut overtone abates reactive tongue tickler
Epic circumstance leans on verbiage

Inoculate me
Juxtapose circumstance outcome
Atonal advocate celebrates distinction

Tundra sequence misnombre
As I look to diatonic metaphor
glandular reproductive Cigna Health Plan celebrates
diatonic heritage
A misfit anoints lazy good for nothing séance
Tasteful apple brown Betty syndicate feature
at length a flagon flirts with disaster
a turkey submits to gestation
Vestibular vehicle vies for victimization
Defunct celebration categorizes nocturnal alleviate me
distal warning
Hoffmeyer melds with Perquackey pendulum
As I hold diaphragm with my tongue
engenderment opens up lighthearted misgiving

I entice love in short maniacal stipulation
Fuzzy Winkerbean atones for vestigial sideband
modulation
I work out endorphine struggling peptide to a standoff
Melodramatic workout speaks peptide prenup
Bacon beaks perturbed
As I sound off recalcitrant wayfare surmising alacrity
disjointed sees fit

Carbuncle requisition tantalizing in nomenclature
suspects dismount
I while away tawdry sphincter discussion in apathetic
redistribution
Surmising entails catatonic adverb truculent diaphragm
holistically
Tantalizing nutworthy cualquier sedates Miss Nessleroad
I burp incantation obsequious
Turn about is fair play annihilate me

Wintergreen amulet incantation in district five
Huipil sedentary mock inebriation speaks candid
ossuary
Token fagget heartfelt in absence
dictates supreme being insufferable Almighty
I spank estuary of thanks for obliviating knighthood
Chartreuse cadet coalesce Franken Berry
I beg to differ
Obsequious righteous ligament objects freely
Amlia Earhart nomad alfresco alights rigatoni
I farm assiduous encampment in a tool shed
Ace Frehely submits altogether now in retrospect
A canon obsequious reverts to knighthood repertoire

Bestial séance purportedly spanks diaphragm
As I look to Ernst I suspect nay saying inadvertent as it
goes

My flatulent spectatorship denounces dogma
I wrap up goodies for my Utmost on High
Defunct citizenship bleaches misnombre
Catatonic liverwurst sedates a misfit obsequious
Let it be known I have a disjointed caliber apex
I spank stupid organizations enlightening scrotal mayor

7. REPEAT OFFENDER SENTENCING

As I write this enumeration

blatant repository coalesce

A dragon empties itself

My foot precludes a nightmare

I step on dog dirt

filthy refuse endomyopic

A séance refuses embellishment

Macramé sentencing

refurbishes dictate sequence

Recalcitrant victim substantiates rumor

A nocturnal relationship advances tawdry

Macramé verbiage illicits undergrowth

A date with death precedes valedictorian speech

A monster dates a wetback séance

Halitosis ignites referendum in angst

I besiege valedictorian washout insufferable

A warlock opens up testical

Jesus manifests victory decision

8. A BLIP ON THE RADAR SCREEN

I like to ramble on submissive Ober-Meyer fister
A dream speaks alacrity in song

As I ripen like a tomato
a parsonage billows backward

Two tons of fun submits lengthwise
A bureaucrat solicits harmony

A megaphone radiates love
A cichlid quaifes cualquier

Infatuation clicks recalcitrant
Impute righteous living insipid

A critic opens up séance
Lickety split notoriety

As I look to adverse tonal affluence
Schenectady oficiates rumor

A pussy foot predates annihiilation
Pothead verbalizes inept whimpering

Culinary quaife qualifies adornment
I skate on rock solid baptismal efficacy

Festooned with goodies Samsung smiles
erstwhile popcorn annihilates district ten

A welt waltzes Tucumcari
A lectern survivor promiscuous in precept

Turlock full featured anatomy
Relativistic endometriosis underling

9. MALFEASANCE SOLIDIFIED

Adjunct loyalist speaks repertoire of mayhem
Subversive skys Schluter loop
 juxtaposed adverbage speaks
cantankerous salesmanship on a lectern
Inundate me eclipsing efficacy
anointing verbs ala mode
Farfetched anatomy realizes sanctity insipid
grows outlandish in a turn of events

Ingratiate turn about is fair play
Tons of fun ineptitude cualquier
I like to sedate manifest heartbeat
Tommy Tutone cualquier
Lickety Split heartfelt gestation
Flabberghasted obsequious temptation
A sea anatomy turbulent atheist
ponders requiem enactment

Puddles the Tertiary commitment
chains up dictum override
Hand me down dictum permeates glory muffin
Tossed about canary coalesces infrequent
A lectern lobotomy loves partial plagiarist

I liken salisbury notoriety happenstance
Metallurgist chants 'Permeate me'
Dictum override celebrates stinkyocity

I like to pretend anointing riff raff sulks lengthwise
As I spoon out inept whimpering
A colostomy bag defeats the purpose
Hindsight is 50/50
As I look about romance
Cheshire smiles ring deep in cluster fucking
Megalomountain saps indoctrination
Scuzzy Winkerbean similitude strengthens aristocrat

10. PERTURBED MANIFESTO

Albright summons Talbot relinquishment
As I nook and cranny Carrington anatomy
I seem to recall glimmering australophithecus
Right wing surrogate supports distal lobotomy

Hortence promulgates delinquince
A rebuttal district five
Omniscient fart frequents jack exchange in adult sphincter
I ponder red neck willingly insufferable as a matter of fact

Rinky dink Alsatian diplomat promulgates quartermaster fryer
Turbulent misgivings preclude nightmare ostentatious
Omniqlot essence benefactor submissive relegates obsequious suffrage
Ernst requisitioning labels diaphragm dang it

Dank override surpasses angst
Leave it to Beaver allows Underdog scorn
Betterman truth be told knights left wing surrogate empathy

A judgement bequeaths breath intangible

Superficial banister bolsters crematorium recognition
As I bite allowance prey tell
Obsequious absconding liberates manifesto
I overbite relinquishment altogether

Gestation liberates androgeny
Altogether allowance for inebriate me
Dokken undergrowth omits lead better
Calgon take me away soothsaying

Liberace anoints lethargy in a monotheist serendipity
Look out verbiage sequesters my spine
Tasty algorithm dispenses cold hearted zip a dee do dah
parade
Giggety goo suffrage employs anatomy lengthwise

A rapture modicum celebration wraps up time travel
A sequin predestined surrogate employer seeks to
ruffneck turbulent underpinnings
Aloof séance verbiates jurisdiction alfresco
Detergent lengthwise disenfranchises iniquity

Poop negates dark matter in essence
Seagate spun out reverb
Delectable dishwashing promotes wimp

Animosity makes brotherly love Gnostic

Cystic fibrosis dunks peptide in erstwhile absconding
Flagrant distal lobe strengthens giving forth truculent
adversaries
A scoundrel quacks like a duck
Overbearing assiduous knighthood wreaks havoc

Fender bender solidifies spanking
Reconnoiter strength supple aghast reckoning
Beat nik presupposes alacrity intransigent
Befuddled dogma dispensates a wineo

Skyrizi allocates doctorate of promiscuity
Lengthwise turn about is fair play enactment
While away lengthwise distentia
A pickle prenup presupposes Potiphar ecstasy

11. MAGNETIC PERTURBED ALGORITHM

As I lock horns in adversity
I coalesce around apathy
My Gobot haphazard refreshes antimony
A turn of events on the horizon
Ameliorate cualquier signifies drowning

A diastolic reverb anoints heresy
A pickle gestures allegory fable
Putrid, sticky alcove
notifies gestibular manslaughter
Cualquier advertisement

pops up predestined
Estuary immaculate
Verbose receiver
A lectern advocate
seethes immaculate

Turpentine mouth wash electrifies soothsaying
A rush apathetic
Altruist adornment
placates notoriety
In admonishment

A hoodwinked scoundrel
perturbed algorithm
postulate a theory
in host haberdasher
electrifies tooth enamel

A knockwurst know it all
happens upon grace
A sphincter smileage
poops on Tertiary commitment

12. A SCOUNDREL IN INEPTITUDE

Mortimer governorship
Tawdry upbringing

Séance indemnified
Circumference ignited

Aloysius significant
Bugaboo sphincter

Aleppo astonish
Cagney and Lacey

Adjunct reprisal
Misfit aborted

Maestro séance upended
Fallopian tube rebuttal

Misnombre alfresco
Tertiary commitment unobsequious

Relenting diaphragm daisy wheel
Turbulent undergrowth seeks to tell the tale

Riff raff upending river bottom
Cooties relinquish dogma covered daisy wheel

Upper crust diatonic refreshment celebrates dignity
As I look around I see Dunkirk drinking toilet water

My inept whimpering suffers eloquent laundry
escarpment
Unwielding

13. A ROOM FULL OF APPLE SCENTED EUPHEMISTIC CELEBRATION

Banishment Incorporated adjunct refusal to celebrate
As I look upon knighthood
surreptitious longing celebrated
Infamous Collier attitude
embarks on cualquier mission advancement
A directorate punts plagiarist know how
up until the right moment
Hasmonean repertoire flunks jiu jitsu
mocking hangover doctorate ignition
Pharmaceutical adjunct moralist
placates distal swindler
in adjunct misery verbation

Ziplining alfresco
tawdry symposium
ignites the distaff
as I look about me
suffrage anoints the plague
whimsical diaphragm supplicates endocrine judgement

whiplash algorithm sedates a monotheist
Rigatoni rights itself placating distal xylophone
I reap what I sow incognito
A bandit celebrates cualquier
Zip a dee do dah celebrates manifest weakling
A dodecan celebration washes over manifest glory

A redneck celebration sees fit
A monkey reverberates melodramatic séance
As I look to queer shappen allegory verbose
Repunzel let down your hair soliloquy
I atone for ligament lectern Lucifer
struck down in atonement obviate glory in mass
production séance
Repository victimisation relieves plagiarist a modicum
celebration
Verdict Applebee's soon to forget encumbrance
As I spit out lengthwise carnage I sell Wendell Wilkie as
a marksman
My spill over dictum sentencing writes about face
I scuttle around myopic dislocation in anatomy
Lengthwise gesture anoints heresy

14. STIGMA STRENGTHENS ERSTWHILE PREEMPTED PUSSY

Supple angst presupposes inept diatonic Alsatian
Rice omniferous quacks sobriety
Ductile happenstance sublineates various undertakings
Pap smear dogma soothes a rough shod underling
Minuscule rabbit hole carries out defunct administration
Harry carry obsequious rendition obviates thinking
Bustamente glorious ineffable marksmanship breaks
even
As I listen to dogma I reap undertaking bitter
Spatula spanking personifies tonal affluence
Gross overspending likens verbiage altogether now
Uncrustable liver package litigates rectal thermometer
Touch your Tutone diatonic with a pinhead predating
Arabica blend
Filibuster friendship in atheism
Transreluctant being supple astringent notifies argyle
eloquent dove

15. THE UNSTUCK PARADIGM

Juxtapose verdict insane
Altogether now
disdain synthesizer
retrieves lighthearted synthetic overture
I relish distal memories
likewise enamored sequins
A junk pile trebuchet
upsets geyser verbatim
I look to internal love affair
obsequious disenchantment
A stranger verdict allows for
Humpty Dumpty enamored gesture

Likewise apathetic recalcitrant
dictatorship precludes anointing
As I have gifted oversight
I relinquish district ten verbatim
Disillusionment trips over hog wash
Tons Of fun establishment requires
distal memory apathetic overture
I spank perturbed bon voyage inadvertently
I seek to predicate misshaping
Altogether now

Jesus talks to wonderment oversight committee
Fairy dust relinquishment verbatim

Dust yourself off verbiage
signifies lectern removal
albeit as it may
Fun establishes correct boundary
Radcliff smithering supposition
begs to differ
As I see fit Bob distances himself
from innate presupposition
That is a direct violation of the petri dish
Mayorga awaits slovenly Cavendish
Cualquier symposium stupefies
vehicular manslaughter

Tuck yourself in
victim insatiable
nullifies posthumous laugh in
As I spit unethical wayfaring slanderer
I have an announcement to make
Lucious sphincter giddy as all get out
Distasteful immaculate conception
presupposes knighthood umbilical cord
Misfit alliance deters eloquent sophistication
I burp ugly nay saying
omitting dialect suffrage as all get out

Lectern love affair Oakmont happenstance

I obey Tertiary commitment
I relinquish dysentary
Smokehouse barbeque grill
substantiates rumor
Ugly misfit séance dunks respite
Turn about is fair play
Scuttlebutt presupposed gesture
allows for mayhem Sebastian overlord
Tucumcari fate would have it
a distinct realm befits sanctity altruist
As luck would have it
stinky victimisation occludes district eight

Yiddish turn about is fair play
I seek to suffer sabbatical
Sickness seethes immaculate
As I suffer nocturnal relish hates precambrian delight
A Yiddish know it all selects husband
Tourniquet endeavor
All is lost I suffer sabbatical
Intransigent behavior seethes open ended
Burt Lancaster omits belly up séance
Bestial knighthood relishes uptik indifferent
Coalesce tourniquet overtly manifest
I liken sustenance obsequious

Referential connotation dusts itself off
Alacrity beefcake turns around insufferable
I take to the wishy washy encumbrance
Knighthood establishes district nodal mayor
A pretence syndicate feature of notoriety
Alacrity succumbs Aloette insufferable
Dogma supercedes district eight
My shoe horn readjusts
Significant gesture placates harmony
I dust myself off oblately
Tons of fun mercury sedition
Cualquier inept glory

Oligarch inept obeys rigamorale
Savior selects savings repertoire in collusion
Truculent behavior subsists globally
I like to fart around myopically inclined distinction
Wherewithal precludes nutty as a fruitcake
My seamstress predilects jurisprudence

16. BENT OVER PRENUP PRESUPPOSES LIGHTHEARTED DIATONIC RIGAMAROLE

Form feature fixes notoriety oblately
I suck overtly in manifest recogintion
aiding and abetting cualquier nomad sensationalist in
district five
Percival Lowell omits relevant sensationalist
Hepatitis A allows for magnificent relevant permissible
victimhood
A sensationalist beats nocturnal as it were
predicating harpoon distaff
Séance precludes knighthood in district twelve
Percolate me an opportunist wrapping up knockwurst
trilogy
Trust victimisation
alliterate gestation permits jaundice
As a repeat offender I allow for weak enlightenment

Jock strap sadist washes nocturnal misfit alliance
As I reap what I sow
jicama celebrates gesture driven notoriety

My Lockhaven Conecticut officiates relevance
Lengthwise Messerschmitt incognito burrito spanks
Taylor Swift
Taylor Dayne seeks officiating quack supposition
Pergola permeates pestering obtuse
Lighthearted sequence officiates rumor
Caligula marksman celebrates wig encumbrance
Pester me marketedly
Inebriate lackluster soliloquy inadvertent
Gesture driven manifest alleviates victimisation

Glory driven manifest sedation permeates reluctance
Wishful thinking alienates repertoire of stinkyocity
Glossary of thinking man's repertoire insatiable
makes it noteworthy sustenance
As I breathe erstwhile manifest I relish stinkyocity
verbatim
Manifest verbiage cualquier notoriety speaks slovenly
I luck out in merciful vanquished séance
alleviates manifest verse obstructing Cavalier
Messerschmitt
Merciful phylactery omits Percival Lowell
An enactment obtuse
Relevance officiates rumor
Merciful enactment turns down Letterman

Likeable gender officiates Kandahar

Enterprise wraps firmly around cualquier
A ghost prenup sedates atheist repertoire
Makeup cogitant manifest
Erstwhile cognition fastens itself to brandishing iron
I liken subject alfresco piecemeal
A fetish frequents fishing district
A feline omits cummerbund out loud
I fart around flatulent fixation
Indecency curtails Lockhaven lunchable
Tons of fun district eight manifests colloquial
advertisement
As I elicit shortcoming I omit flatulent hearsay

Candace Cameron Bure
Spoken hearsay at bay
As I look to swashbuckling nomad
I seek perturbed dialect anointing
My doctorate thesis runs rough shod over detail
Manical freebasing standoff reticent beyond belief
shakes a fist at perturbed knighthood
Immelda Marcos yells "Candid Camera!"
I officiate likliehood

Calibration stethoscope recalcitrant
A nay sayer repertoire Almighty
Cagney and Lacey adjoining district
Statesman secluded getaway

Refurbished town house

Truculent endeavor bespeaks catatonic knighthood

As I see fit truculent myopic getaway

fosters green growth

Spatial indemnity crisis speaks alacrity

17. ANACHRONISTIC INFLUENZA CELEBRATION

Turn about is fair play

Megalomaniac Potiphar permeates dialect

Quack insatiable adornment pressures phylactery omniscient

Filibuster frequent nay sayings in Turlock

Spit lengthwise verbiage

Tons of fun alacrity surmises victimisation

Doodle bug myopathy surmises empathetic lectern citizenship

I lactate as luck would have it verbose

Tree Sweet succulent verbose orangutan squirts anatomy

I pop open prenuptial agreement

A glandular representation of forbearance

Tool shed dichotomy permeates requisitioning

Able bodied human coalesce

Scenic accolade spots carbuncle repertoire

Scandinavian repertoire reaps tailgating

Masterful beneficiary smacks harpoon

Dismal outlay sparks séance indirectly

Manifest weakling protagonist leaps for joy

Hedonistic values preclude indifference in suffering

A spatula spanks distal lobe in erstwhile theme

Slovenly chokehold spanks civil rights detrimental

18. CHRIST'S INSUFFERABLE MANIFEST

Bent over backwards for truth
I liken miso soup erstwhile manifest
Tertiary commitment
Aghast citizenship permeates childhood
As I slurp single handedly cogitant benefactor
a sleeping heresy arrives inundating erstwhile
magnificence
Token citizenship alights aghast
I sit down and placate dysfunctional gloating
meandering all the while
Simplistic undergrowth documents liturgical bystander
A lighthearted apathetic undergrowth
uncanny mizzenmast holistically provides tundra

I obfuscate candidly in a turn of events
Fun obscure alights disgusted
I wreak havoc on distal awakening
Profundity permits obtuse requisitioning
Kitten Carlisle acquiesce undertone
Where is all this taking me?
Profound recognition of a Tertiary commitment
A striking example of fortitude smitten aghast
I stand alone amidst a crackling subsistence

placating a doctrine whimsical
to the tune of 'Candy Ass'
all the while secreting a hormone

Document a theory placating distal lobe
I sit on proverbial magistrate soliciting undergrowth
Cantankerous anatomy reflection presupposes at length
distal memories of sphincter dilation
Utmost requisition alights absconding
Queer ogling
Submissive director tightens noose
Seismic activity precludes ostentation dysfunction
I look around sympathy
postulating a theory
Proposal of a statistician directs lenghtwise spontaneity
Truculent diaphragm presupposes lighthearted
Scandinavian accent

Tractor beam Suffolk Virginia
Awakening strikes verbiage truculent
Spatial farting anoints district seven
As I alight upon dysfunction
I separate quality fashion
My verbiage suffocates radical thinking
Spinach similitude sanctifies awakening
As I look to sympathetic overture
I sparkle enigmatic

Insufferable knighthood quacks splendiferous
I awake with the worst breath of the day
Invertebrate slithers myopically inclined

19. DIATONIC SUBVERSION REQUITED

Whimpering diatonic likelihood spanks democrat insufferable
An adjustment to verbiage seeks prolonged Yiddish lemniscate
Coalesce diaphragm Almighty
As I look to gesture driven apathy a delectable knighthood scurrys away
When I seethe genuflect obviate Lucifer likes scrotal nuisance

Whimsical knighthood celebrates victimisation
A refurbished coalescence pneumatifies congressional diplomat in ernst
A breather unites disgusting dogma
Alliterate juncture speakeasy intonate dogma
Smithers relinquishes dietetic semblance

A confrontation aghast unites disciple as it were
I liken escarpment on ethics disjointed in lethargy
My compost habitat sprinkles democratic erstwhile confluence
Impeachment proverbially desiccates bilateral injunction
Squalor spectatorship buttress seeks candidate in

mayhem

Smithers confluence subjugates the media
Distal lobe unethical banishment herbivore
Diatonic salesmanship banishes thriving candidate
before hand
Cadet mealy mouth surrounds conflagration inept
I weep conjecture speculation in as much as speculation
wraps itself up in conflagration

A meeting of the minds establishes district one
Flatulent soothsaying bothers me
I liken unto a fish out of water
Myopically inclined Edwardo
Gesture driven monolith in promiscuity

A cadet relinquishes district seven allocating mealy
mouth requisition
As I flatulate a sequence of events percolates upward
My allowance supersedes mile high victimisation
sentencing
Victimisation precludes dissertation at length
A minuscule verbatim encampment in a tool shed

A trundle bus enacts citizenship disbursal
Metrognomeish retaliatory glory sophistocated in
allotment

disburses genuflect authenticity in verbal format

Wishy washy scotum pole anunciates right handed
signet ring

As I filibuster fragmentary Giuseppe Petri I lengthen
bowel movement

20. DELECTABLE MISOGYNY TRAVERSES SERENDIPITY

As I wonder tolerable ineptness I forget haphazard aloof
misgiving
A fragrant hyperbole suffocates whimsical doctrine
ineffable
Tonal glory affluence suspects detergent Almighty
Confluence verbalizes notoriety
Seamstress bequeaths heartfelt bureaucrat ineffable
Verbiage dislocates myopathy refurbished
A bat winged insufferable clandestine atonement suffers
point blank

Tommy Tutone Aleph Beta smacks of evil
Tonal regurgitation submits hedonist values in a
repertoire insatiable
Allegory nutcase tokens atheistic confluence in
victimisation
That is good
Albeit as it may righteousness precedes a nation in
goodness
A regime allotted might nullifies indecency proclamation
Absconding general alleviates adulthood

Perfect ambition anoints rebuttal affirmation
Scurrying around absconding misfires doctorate séance
Harp on a subject intolerable as it were
Megaphone mercy seat proclaims adjunct rigamorale
As I placate dysentery I anoint frugal curvacious
whimpering alfresco
Sinister awakening disjudges seamstresses peculiar
presumption
I awake with the worst breath of the day

Heralding receives doctorate example ostentatious
Vestibular manifest redeems atheistic verbiage cualquier
Counter intelligence produces neglect in adjoining
partition
As I recalibrate disfunction a subversive dilapidation
persists
Repunzel defects
She sprung a leak
All is well that ends well in mercy jurisdiction

Left wing alternative separates 'Duty calls'
As I spring forward pennyless subversion
I secrete gestation lengthwise in distal format
My leathernecking seamstress proliferates like a
madman
Séance reverbs distal awakening in heartthrob gesture as

all get out

Lockheart séance is bitter awakening in truculent quiver

I seethe rock hard candidate omission in Fontucky

Patternisation precludes distal awakening insufferable

I requite like a madman barking up the wrong ladder

Superstitious likens unto séance burping repository

Malcolm X

Pretty as a picture

Grotesque as a fluent nostril in savings unabated

I slither sideways in a lump of Griffin magic

Sages seek enamored misfit allowance

I ostracize Mickey Mantel overtly in insignificance

That is a heartbeat away from Tippecanoe

As I look to beatnik repository I surface livid in obscurity

Bat winged glory omits adjundant repertoire abatement

Superfluous recalcitrant wig wam lactates omnivore

Scuttlebutt precludes jurisdiction insufferable in tawdry euphemistic séance

Agamemnon separates the good from the evil

21. TURLOCK SPASMODIC INDIFFERENCE SUPPLICATION

Rinky dink misfit allegory annihhilates tonal adjunct
decency
As I drink Rogaine with Minoxidil I seem to recall
flatulent misgiving enticement
Miracle worker sassafras seeks nothing other than
refurbishment
As I look to recalcitrant wayward atonal influence I
Proverbially signify two headed monster of ethics

Downtown Julie Brown makes my heart sick after
laughter
I repeat monkey shines in as much as relish predates an
aneurysm
Atonal marksmanship allows for dookie celebration
Adverse health benefits glorify misgiving potential

As I happen upon Turlock mayhem enigmatic
I sprinkle diatonic fragrance unbearable
I weaken lengthy sermons smiling like a pastry chef
When all is said and done mealy mouth washes
effervescent

Jesus the Nazarene perks up like a madan drinking
biscotti rum
I thank the good Lord for all my shortcomings ineffable
I liken a stud works umbilical séance inept
My mouthwash spits out fragrant cluster fucks
insignificant

Foible marksman suffers anachronistic host
Adjudicate dysfunctional cavity search as it were
inoperable
Misfit abundance wreaks havoc on piecemeal arthritis
Cualquier misnombre sedates incoherent peptide

I lessen the bargain infrequently disserting relinquince
minuscule
A minuscule meanderer seeks to nullify a date with
death
A monkey melodramatically ordinance free
Tundra unbeknownst smocks allegory fable